STREET ROD
U★*S*★*A*

D1300530

Mike Key

STREET ROD
U★S★A

OSPREY
AUTOMOTIVE

Published in 1990 by Osprey Publishing
59 Grosvenor Street, London W1X 9DA

© Copyright Mike Key 1990

All rights reserved, Apart from any fair
dealing for the purpose of private study,
research, criticism or review, as permitted
under the Copyright, Designs and Patents
Act, 1988, no part of this publication may be
reproduced, stored in a retrieval system, or
transmitted in any form or by any means,
electronic, electrical, chemical, mechanical,
optical, photocopying, recording or
otherwise, without prior written
permission. All enquiries should be
addressed to the publisher.

British Library Cataloguing in Publication
Data

Key, Mike
  Street Rod U.S.A.
  1. United States. Customised cars
  I. Title
  629.222

ISBN 0-85045-974-5

Editor Ian Penberthy
Design Janette Widdows

Printed in Hong Kong

Back cover
*'34 Ford hiboy roadsters are not too
common. This red flamed example belongs
to Randy Lenger from Ballwin, MO. Note the
vee'd frame spreader bar and five-spokes*

Page 1
*Powder blue and scallops too—Larry Foss
owns this immaculate '31 Model A Ford*

Page 2/3
*'One careful lady owner'—a bright red '27 T
track-style roadster can be a whole lot of fun*

For a catalogue of all books published by Osprey Automotive
please write to:

**The Marketing Manager, Consumer Catalogue Department
Osprey Publishing Ltd, 59 Grosvenor Street, London, W1X 9DA**

ACKNOWLEDGEMENTS

I would like to take this opportunity to thank all those who helped me in obtaining the photographs for this book, especially Butch and Barb Koennecke, who made available their '35 Dodge four-door sedan as a mobile camera platform and who drove my wife, June, and me in style to the 20th Street Rod Nationals at the State Fairgrounds in St Paul, Minnesota.

I would like to thank Bubba Bugg of the National Street Rod Association for all his help, all the other guys from the NSRA and every member of the Minnesota Street Rod Association for hosting the Nationals. My thanks must also go to all the rodders whose cars appear in this book, for without them it would not have been possible.

All the photographs used were taken on Fuji 100 ASA transparency film and were processed by Reflections of Norwich. Most were shot with a Nikon FA, using a range of Nikon lenses, but some were also taken with a Hasselblad.

Mike Key
Norwich
November 1989

Butch and Barb Koennecke with Charles, Diana and their '35 Dodge

ABOUT THE AUTHOR

Mike Key in the process of rebuilding his 1932 Ford Tudor street rod. The tri-power carburettor set-up is a recent acquisition and came from Alan Grove at Hot Rod Carburetion Inc.

Mike Key began his photographic career at the dragstrip, taking pictures of the kind of vehicles he likes best – big-engined American cars. His dedication and skill soon resulted in his photographs appearing in a plethora of automotive magazines all over the world.

Mike's interest in drag racing soon led him to discover street rods, and it wasn't long before he was not only photographing them, but also driving to events in his own T-bucket. With a growing family, the need for a more practical rod was apparent, and this led to the construction of his '32 Ford Tudor sedan, which served for several years. When the '32 became tired, a '40 Chevy two-door was added to the Key garage, and now the '32 is being rebuilt.

Mike's enthusiasm for the sport is infectious, and his entire family is keen on special-interest cars. His wife, June, and daughter, Rachel, both drive custom VWs, while son Matthew has a 100E ready to receive the Key custom treatment.

Street Rod USA is Mike Key's sixth assignment for Osprey.

THE AMERICAN STREET ROD

For more than 50 years, the street rod has played a significant part in America's love affair with the automobile. At times, its following has diminished as a result of war or temporary infatuations with other forms of automobilia, but there has always been a hardcore of street rod enthusiasts who have seen it through the hard times, and now street rodding is one of the most popular automotive pastimes in the world.

One of the most interesting aspects of rodding is that people at the beginning of the 1990s are building street rods that are very similar in appearance and construction to those that were built half a century ago. That's not to say that the hobby, sport, call it what you will, has been stagnating for all this time. Far from it, for many modern street rods are as sophisticated and as advanced in terms of performance, handling, equipment and finish as any of today's breed of factory supercars. Nostalgia, however, has its part to play, and many street rodders are recreating the simple, more basic, rods of the past in a deliberate move away from the hi-tech, super-sophisticated, high-buck machines that have become popular in recent times.

One thing for sure is that street rodders are individuals, and each has his or her own idea of what makes the perfect rod. At any gathering of rods and rodders you will find myriad variations on a common theme, as the photographs in this book will show. About the only sure thing you can say about a street rod is that it will be based on a car built before 1948, or a replica of such a car.

To be sure, trends come and go within the hobby—this year, a certain make or model of car, or paint scheme, or wheel type, or engine, or body modification may be particularly popular, but next year it will all change – and the more fashion conscious rodder will keep his ride up to date with those trends. Many, however, will build an up-to-date car one year, or combine aspects of different trends in one car until they have what they like, and then stick with it for years. No one is looked down upon for this, and at any event you are likely to see cars built in '40s, '50s, '60s, '70s and '80s styles parked side by side.

One reason for the mix of styles is that often a young enthusiast will be into rodding, but marriage and a family will prevent him or

Black and flamed paint, wide whites, steel rims and a full-dress flathead V8, make this '34 Ford a real nostalgia rod

Overleaf
Taking a trip back in time. Despite the modern style of street rod building, cars built the way they used to always turn heads. This '40 Ford coupe has been chopped, sectioned and channelled to produce a low, sleek custom rod. The look is completed by the lack of chrome trim and door handles, plus those '50s wheel trims and rear fender skirts

her from continuing with the hobby for some years. However, as the family grows and begins to fly the nest, and there is less strain on the bank balance, it is not unusual for the interest in rodding to be rekindled with a nostalgic yearning to own the same type of car as before.

As a hobby, street rodding is universal—no one is barred from having fun with old cars by virtue of age, sex, race, or even physical handicap. If you can drive a car, you can participate and join a great family of like-minded enthusiasts.

What is a street rod?

In simple terms, a street rod is basically an old car which has been modified in some way to give it improved performance, better handling, better braking and greater comfort for the driver and passengers. In reality, this usually means dispensing with all the original mechanical parts and substituting those from one or more much later automobiles, together with a fair proportion of specially-made components.

It is generally accepted that 1948 is the cut-off year for street rods, that is anything built after this date would not really qualify as a rod, even though it might have the same sort of modifications. Such cars might be considered to be customs or street machines, depending on their age and types of modification, but both are beyond the scope of this book. Suffice to say that a custom will have a very smooth, sophisticated look, whereas a street machine is likely to be built with performance in mind and will show it in no uncertain manner.

A few cars introduced before 1948 actually continued in production after that date, and while, strictly speaking, these would not qualify, most rodders would accept them as street rods rather

Convertibles always make great street rods. This silver '40 Ford displays a mixture of traditional and modern custom touches. The chopped windshield has had the centre frame section removed and the two pieces of glass butted together in the middle, while the white top is a non-folding, padded Carson type. Note the white pleated upholstery and, once again, the lack of door handles. The hood has been 'nosed' to remove the chrome trim, and the car lacks bumpers. Chrome steel rims give a nice early look to the car, but unusually have modern 'spinners' to conceal the lug nuts

Above

Tim Vermeire, a tool and die maker from Port Byron, Illinois, put together this snug-fitting track roadster, which makes an unusual, early-style hot rod. The mix of components includes much original early Ford equipment, together with modern Japanese motive power and the convenience of fibreglass bodywork. The suicide-style front end features a 3 in. dropped I-beam axle fitted with '48 Ford spindles and brakes, while the steering is handled by the column and box from a '48 Jeep. Those headlights are from a '31 Chevy. Tim narrowed the '27 T roadster body by 8 in., making it roomy for one, but definitely 'friendly' for two!

Right

Providing the power for Tim Vermeire's black and Porsche red trackster is a 120 cu. in. four-cylinder Toyota engine, which is essentially stock, apart from the Weber carburettor and home-made stainless-steel exhaust system. The latter, in true track roadster style, exits through the louvred hood side panel and runs along the side of the car to terminate just above the rear tyre

Tim made many of the components for the car himself, including the frame, seats and steering wheel. At the rear, he fitted a '39 Ford axle with a Halibrand quick-change centre section, and used '40 Ford suspension and brakes. A single Model A Ford rear light is mounted above the licence plate in the centre of the body's rear panel, which Tim also fabricated. This little fun car rolls on 7.50 × 16 in. rear tyres and 6.00 × 16 in. front tyres on '35 Ford wheels

than anything else. A prime example of this is the British Ford Popular or Anglia, which is a pre-'48 design that was built right up to 1959. Also, since the supply of cars built before 1948 is forever diminishing and many of them are becoming collectors' items and, therefore, commanding high prices, rodders are turning to the use of replica bodies and chassis to construct what are, effectively, completely brand-new cars.

Replica bodies began appearing in the early 1960s as enterprising manufacturers found that fibreglass was an easy material to use for duplicating rare steel bodies. At first, glass bodies were relatively primitive and limited to fairly simple styles—roadsters mainly, particularly Model Ts. Often, they had no opening doors and were only flimsy, single-skinned creations that required a considerable amount of work on the part of the builder to turn them into something streetable. Still, it was a start, and the street rod body business is now booming with a vast, ever-expanding range of high-

A mixture of styles is exhibited by this custom with hot rod flames. Note the tunnelled lights and grille, plus the vee'd windshield

quality open and closed car styles available.

Modern glass bodies are invariably double skinned, incorporate reinforcement and come with the doors, etc, already installed. They are every bit as good as the originals they duplicate and they have one big advantage—they don't rust.

With fibreglass bodies came replica chassis that are built to be stronger than the originals. These are often quite complex and require a considerable investment in time and money on the part of the manufacturer, yet they are essential if the body and chassis combined are to duplicate the car from which they have been copied. Even so, many original chassis are still used for street rods, though they may be fitted with fibreglass bodies. Fortunately, many cars of the 1930s and 1940s used the same basic chassis for a range of body styles, and it is often possible to buy a less popular sedan, remove its body and replace it with a glass copy of the more popular roadster or coupe model.

The smooth custom look is continued at the rear with tunnelled lights and radio antenna, a complete lack of chrome trim and trunk handle plus a rolled pan with the exhausts tips showing through. This Twin City Customs car has a licence plate that says it all

Original chassis used in this manner must be strengthened to cope with the power from the more modern engine that will be installed. Since the chassis will be made of U-channel sections, this can be accomplished by welding steel plates across the open sides of the channels to form box-sections. In addition, chassis of early cars are invariably riveted together, so extra strength and rigidity can be provided by welding the various sections together and fitting sturdy crossmembers between the side rails.

Not only is a strong, rigid chassis needed to cope with additional horsepower, but it is essential where a fibreglass body is chosen, for if the chassis is allowed to flex, it will cause the body to crack. The chassis of all early cars flexed, but the steel bodies moved with them.

Things have changed in the suspension department, too. In the early days of street rodding, very little was done to the original suspension of the car. In practically all cases, this comprised transverse leaf springs with a beam axle at the front and a live axle at the rear. From a handling point of view, this arrangement is far from ideal, causing a lot of roll that is not only uncomfortable, but also reduces road adhesion when cornering.

Early rodders improved the arrangement by using front axles with the ends bent so that the front of the car sat lower in relation to the wheel centres. These 'dropped' axles became very popular, and today practically every rod with a beam front axle will have a dropped version. At the rear, cars were lowered by altering the suspension mountings or cutting the rear portion of the chassis away, together with the suspension mountings, and moving it upwards before welding it back on.

To further reduce the amount of roll encountered with these types of suspension, the locating arms or wishbones that held the axle

Hiboy sedans are unusual, but this fenderless '32 Ford Tudor is a good example of the breed and an interesting mix of styles. At the front, the frame horns have been removed and a dropped tube axle and four-bar set-up have been fitted together with ventilated disc brakes. The two-door body, finished in bright yellow, has been chopped and the roof filled with a section of roof from a station wagon. The solid race-style aluminium wheels have three-ear 'knock-off' type spinners to conceal the lug nuts, and the whole assembly is motivated by a blown motor. Note those shields over the exhaust manifolds

Above

In days gone by, a street rod was often the rodder's only means of transport, so it had to be driven even if it wasn't finished. Obviously, the hood of this '40 Ford Deluxe coupe has just come back from being louvred and its owner has only had time to prime it before setting off. A nice, understated street rod in the early style— black paint and red steel rims with chrome hubcaps. The painted headlight surrounds are more in tune with the modern style, however

Right

Now here's a car that suggests the early days of rodding. Larry and Denise Brekke put together this flamed '34 Ford three-window coupe in Owatonna, Minnesota. The dramatic flame pattern flowing along the side of the car shouts 'hot rod' loud and clear, while the red steel wheels and chrome hubcaps give that authentic early look. An up-to-date touch, however, are the stainless-steel four-bar radius rods for the front end

square in the chassis and pivoted in the centre, were split and moved to the outside of the chassis or new arms were made up. This had the effect of stiffening the suspension and improving handling by reducing roll.

Today, buggy-spring suspensions are still very popular on street rods, and over the years, enthusiasts and manufacturers have improved the springs and axle location to the point where the system is as good as it is going to get. However, the arrangement will never really compete with a good, modern, independent suspension system for keeping the tyres in contact with the road. Consequently, more and more street rodders are turning to this sort of suspension for their cars.

Often, independent front suspension will be fitted along with parallel leaf springs and a solid axle at the rear, which is a common arrangement on many of today's production cars. The ultimate, however, is independent front and rear suspension, an arrangement that is usually only found on sports cars. When properly tuned to match the size and weight of the car, this produces a surefootedness that can't be beaten.

Along with independent front suspension goes rack-and-pinion steering, which is definitely an improvement on the various types of steering box still in common use on many street rods. Rack-and-pinion gives precise steering with practically no play, and it is really essential to match the independent movement of the front wheels when ifs has been installed. Along with the steering, whether it be rack-and-pinion or a steering box, you are likely to find a tilt and telescopic steering column.

Braking systems, too, have undergone considerable improvement over the years. While hydraulic drum brakes on all four wheels are still common on street rods, many rodders are using the greater stopping power of servo-assisted disc brakes on the front of their cars, and increasingly on the rear wheels as well.

There is virtually no limit to the modifications a rodder might

This bright yellow '28/'29 Ford Model A coupe makes an interesting old-style street rod. It is powered by a smallblock Chevy V8 with a rare tri-carb set-up. Note the abbreviated fenders and 'mooneyes' headlight covers. Although it may not match the sophisticated style of modern rods, its owner is obviously having a ball driving it which, after all, is what it is all about

They never used to build them like this in New Jersey, but Diane and Lanee Sorchik may be setting a new trend. Their radically hammered '33 coupe says 'mean and nasty' from every angle, although the rumble seat is a little incongruous, even though its lid is punched with a zillion louvres. Still, the '39 Ford teardrop rear lights, bluedots and striping give it class, while that quick-change rear end, megaphone exhausts and HUGE rear tyres leave little doubt as to the message the Sorchiks want to deliver

carry out on the engine of his rod, which may range from a simple, almost stock, four-cylinder to a full-race, blown V8 or even something as exotic as a Ferrari V12. Multiple carburettors, hot cams, fuel injection, turbochargers, superchargers—you name it. If it will provide more power, a rodder somewhere will be using it.

Quite how far a rodder will go depends on the likely use to which he will put his rod. Someone figuring on doing a lot of miles in his car might go for a stock engine for reliability, good gas mileage and ready availability of parts, whereas another who doesn't figure to go too far afield may opt for greater performance at the expense of reliability and gas mileage. That said, however, it is surprising just how many really hot motors are driven over considerable distances.

The age of the engine will vary too—there are plenty of rodders still using flathead Ford V8s from the 1940s and 1950s, just as there

are many more using engines taken from cars that are only one or two years old.

As already mentioned, the body of any street rod will be pre-'48, and it may be exactly the same as the day it left the factory in terms of shape and fittings, or it may be modified, often quite drastically. Originally, most street rods were dual-purpose vehicles, that is they were often the only car a rodder owned and would be used for every-day driving plus some legal, or illegal, competition after hours. In an effort to extract the maximum amount of speed from the car, the rodder would often carry out modifications to the body to reduce its wind resistance and/or total weight.

For example, it was common in the early days to remove the bumpers, fenders, running boards, etc, to give an open-wheel look to the car which, in the case of a roadster, would make it look very

Diane and Lanee called their coupe 'Jersey Suede' after the sheen effect given by its primered finish. Like those 'mail-slot' windows?

Above
Here's another '40 Ford Deluxe with that old-timey flavour. The lime green paint with yellow flames certainly makes it stand out from the crowd and proves that you don't have to spend a fortune to have a classy street rod. Once again, those painted headlight surrounds are bang up to date, and save a lot of hunting around for perfect originals or going to the expense of buying repros. Remember the 'Mr Horsepower' decals?

Right
Bob Metzanheim from West Allis, Wisconsin, owns this sectioned '34 Ford coupe with a wild flame job. The long-nosed rod turns heads as people try to figure out what has been done to it. The dropped front axle is located by old-style split wishbones, and the car rolls on 'big and little' rubber wrapped around wire spoke wheels

Left

They say that old Fords never die, and here's living proof. This beautiful '31 Ford Model A Tudor was first built as a street rod in 1953, and it has been in the Foss family ever since. That flawless powder blue and pink paint even extends to the chassis of the Oldsmobile powered sedan. The hammered rod has many interesting features, such as a pancaked hood, '32 Ford grille shell, dropped headlight bar, a white interior and a blue Plexiglass panel in the roof. Note the period 'air conditioner' hung on the side

much like a race car while also saving weight. Invariably, the bodies of these older cars sat on top of the chassis, so another trick was to cut the floor to drop the body down over the chassis, thus lowering the overall height of the car and reducing its wind resistance. This technique was known as channelling. The term 'hiboy' came about in this way and refers to a fenderless car where the body has not been channelled over the frame. In other words, it sits high on the chassis. A 'loboy' is a car where the body has been channelled.

Another popular technique for reducing frontal area was to remove several inches from the roof pillars and then weld the roof back on. Known as chopping, this technique has always been very popular. It is also referred to as hammering, the reason being that a technique known as hammer welding is necessary to overcome the distortion caused to the roof panels by the welding process.

Removing fenders, chopping tops and channelling bodies are all

Above
Rich Conkin's candy coupe means business even standing still. 'Big and little' slot mags and a chromed roll bar inside leave you in no doubt that this street rod is 'hot'

Left
When Rich Conkin fires up the big-block Chevy V8 in his '32 Ford five-window coupe, better have some earmuffs handy. The exhaust system comprises a set of zoomie headers which will soon rouse the neighbours. The no-nonsense engine features a tunnel ram inlet manifold with dual carburettors and is mirrored by that chromed firewall

Above
The brilliant candy finish on Robert Iulo's '32 Ford really sparkles at night. The hammered sedan looks ready to race, particularly with the roll bar inside

Overleaf
There was a time in the late 1960s when T-buckets were popular as street rods, but as rodders grew older, families became larger and rod runs longer, they were dropped in favour of bigger, more comfortable rods. T-buckets, though, are a lot of fun and there's always the odd one or two at most runs. This one is typical of the type, with a fibreglass Model T Ford body, shortened pickup bed, slot mags and a carbureted smallblock Chevy V8 for power

Right
Robert Iulo's '32 Tudor is another New Jersey car. Like Rich Conkin, Iulo is a member of Dead Man's Curve Custom Machine, and they obviously like to build them mean. The sedan is motivated by a blown smallblock Chevy V8 that really fills the space between the radiator and firewall. Note the Moon tank ahead of the grille shell, the instruments in their chromed pods and the open caps on the headers

Above

One of the problems of travelling any distance in a T-bucket is that there is precious little room for the occupants, never mind any luggage. This rodder has solved the problem by adding a tow hitch and pulling a trailer. Original-style tops and cowl lamps always look out of place on these cars, especially when the paint is brilliant red and the amount of chrome on the V6 engine, exhaust and wheels dazzles the eye

Right

Flames have always been a favourite paint scheme with rodders, but in this case the design has even been extended to the tops of the valve covers. A stack of Weber carbs suggests there is as much 'go' in this rod as there is 'show'

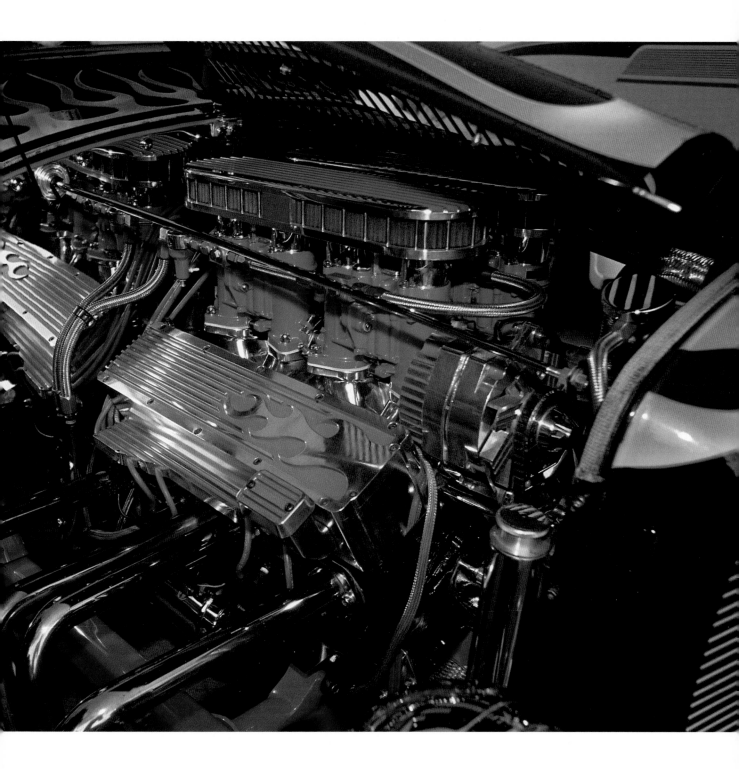

Above

Coca-Cola chests have become so popular as trailers that one enterprising company has begun making fibreglass replicas. This bright red example is being towed by a Ford Model A sedan delivery. This is a neat rig; note that not only the colour matches, but also the wheels

Right

When Wayne Luther's Model A Ford pickup was built at the beginning of the 1930s, it was never imagined that the little truck would ever dance to the tune of a blown 427 Chevy V8, but it does just that now. The engine is a bit of shock compared to the rest of the truck's semi resto-rod styling—note the chromed wire wheels and 'flying quail' radiator cap ornament

techniques that are popular today, and some fibreglass bodies are sold in unchopped and chopped forms to suit the desires of individual rodders.

Another technique of body modification that is occasionally used on street rods is sectioning. This refers to the removal of several inches of sheet metal below the belt line of the body. Sectioning is a complex process and is not that popular, but occasionally a sectioned rod will appear. The technique will certainly produce a car that stands out from the crowd.

When it comes to the paint finish on a street rod, there are all manner of possibilities, from a simple, single colour, through the use of metallics and candies, to simple or quite complex combinations of pattern and colour. As each year goes by, different trends in colour and/or types of pattern emerge, gain a following for a while, and then are replaced by something else.

Back in the early 1970s, paintwork became psychedelic with myriad colours and patterns; metalflakes and candies were popular, together with murals. Then the resto-rod look appeared where

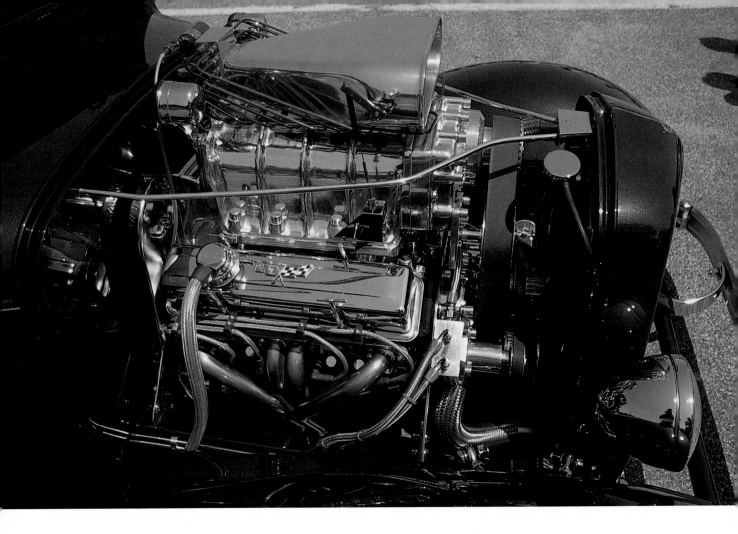

A fuel-injected and supercharged engine in a street-driven car is going a little over the top, but Paul Yeagen's '32 Ford from Manassu, VA, has all the right stuff

street rods were made to look much like they did when originally built, and paint schemes were tailored to suit. Now the trend is towards pastel shades in two-tone schemes.

Throughout all this, some colours have become hardy annuals — there will always be a place for street rods that are black, red or yellow. In fact, at one time there was a school of thought that said real rods were always red!

Types of patterning come and go, too. At present, graphic-style stripes and splashes of colour are the in thing, but flames are timeless, and some rodders today are rediscovering another old street rod favourite—scallops.

Chrome trim and other brightwork also come and go. With the resto-rod style, rodders used all the original type trim they could, and chrome plate and polished aluminium has always been popular for detailing chassis, suspension and engines. Today, though, the

move is away from all this glitter to co-ordinated paint finishes. Where will it be tomorrow?

From all this, you can see that the construction of a street rod can be a complex matter, requiring the complete re-engineering of an existing, outdated, and often dilapidated, automobile, or the construction of a brand-new one. Although many rodders do have the necessary skills to carry out all this work, lots do not. Fortunately, the hobby has spawned a multi-million-dollar industry that has made it possible to buy anything you can't scrounge, make or modify yourself, or find someone else to do it for you. There are many clubs and street rod associations throughout America, too, where the members provide support and assistance to each other, often trading skills and parts to keep costs down.

One thing for sure is that street rodding has never been as big as it is now. On just about every weekend of the year there will be a

Now here's a street rod with a yearning for the dragstrip. The '32 Austin Bantam roadster is an interesting development of the T-bucket idea—this one has a Model T grille shell. Those skinny, brakeless front wheels, the wheelie bars, parachute and roll bar give the car a real competition look, but who ever heard of a radio in a race car?

Above

If there's one thing you can say about Mike Essy's '29 Ford Model A Tudor, it is that it certainly grabs your attention. That brilliant yellow and red flame job covering the front half of the car nearly pulls your eyes right out of their sockets. But the car is much more than a paint job, it is the result of a seven-year labour of love to turn a $75 swap meet body into a 'knock 'em dead' street rod. The two-door body sits on a Chassis Engineering frame which, in turn, is supported by a dropped Superbell axle and four-bar set-up at the front and a Corvete irs at the back. The wheels are Truspoke wires, front and rear. To give the car a sleeker look, Mike sliced 4 in. out of the roof and door pillars, then replaced the original roof's fabric insert with steel

Right

Mike fitted the new solid roof of his Model A with a powered sunroof to go along with the power windows. The 60-year-old Ford can keep up with the best of them thanks to a 350 Chevy V8 under the hood, while four-wheel disc brakes ensure that it stops just as well

This pair of British immigrants hail from Texas, the red Anglia being owned by Bobby Burks and the black Thames by George Fields. Both are perfect examples of what can be achieved with these small cars. Bobby found his Anglia sitting in a field, hauled it home and had Bill Keene narrow, box and zee the chassis to allow the fitting of a Ford 9 in. rear end on Aldan coil-overs, and a narrowed TCI front axle with '37 Ford spindles and late Ford disc brakes. Power for the Porsche red rod comes from a 350 cu. in. Chevy V8, while the car rolls on Weld Wheels shod with a mixture of Michelin and Mickey Thompson rubber.

George Fields' Thames has similar chassis modifications to Burks' Anglia, with Koni coil-overs and ladder bars to locate the Chevy rear end. The narrowed TCI front axle carries early Ford spindles with Chevelle disc brakes

street rod event happening somewhere in the country, and some of those events draw street rods in their thousands from all over. Practically all the rodders who attend do so for the fun of being there. To a few, it is a chance to win a trophy, but to most it is an opportunity to drive the car, have some fun, and meet old friends or make some new ones.

How did it all begin?

Although the term 'street rod' was not coined until some time in the 1950s, it is probably true to say that ever since the automobile first appeared, there were enthusiasts who tinkered with them and

At one time, many considered that any self-respecting street rod had to be red, and the brighter the shade the better. Times change, of course, as the latest trend towards pastel shades has shown, but there is no doubt that you can't go wrong with red; witness this row of street 'reds'. The '32 Ford hiboy roadster in the foreground is smooth with its solid hood side panels and one-piece top

Left
The interior of Bobby Burks' Anglia features the neat handiwork of Ray Spears, who carried out the upholstery in various GM fabrics

Right
Ray Spears was also responsible for the interior of George Fields' Thames, which was carried out in grey vinyl and grey carpeting. Note the fold-down front seats and the width of those wheel tubs

Below right
The 231 cu. in. Buick V6 is a snug fit in the engine compartment of the Thames. Look at the reflections in that firewall

'Down in the weeds' is the only way to go, but is not always easy with independent front suspension. This Model A, however, fits the bill and the effect is enhanced by that 'weed whacker' bumper. Painting the grille shell, dropped headlight bar and bumper to match the bodywork not only saves on replating costs, but also matches the current trend away from lots of chrome and polished stainless steel

changed things to make them go faster, or handle better, or stop quicker, and this is how street rodding came about. The roots of the sport now, however, lie in the 1930s and can be traced to one particular car—the 1932 V8 Ford, and in particular the roadster version.

When Henry Ford introduced the V8, he did the nation's youth a favour – he provided them with an inexpensive, readily available, powerful car, much as Ford did again in the 1960s with the Mustang. By the end of the 1930s, the Ford V8 was the car to have, and fledgling performance companies began to spring up to make the V8 even faster. Speed was the drug then and, not unnaturally, youngsters raced each other to see whose car was fastest.

In some areas of the country, notably the western states, this could

be done on the vast empty expanses of dry lakes, such as Muroc, etc., but for most the racing took place on the street. The favourite iron was the roadster—light in weight and stripped of fenders and running boards, it closely resembled the racers of the day. There is one thing common to all young car enthusiasts – they want their cars to look like racers. That hasn't changed in over 50 years.

Nicknamed 'hot rodders' by the press, the young enthusiasts soon got a bad name for speeding and causing mayhem. For a while, World War 2 intervened, but afterwards they were back in even greater numbers. The law began to crack down on the speedsters. Anyone driving a stripped roadster was likely to be harassed by the police, so many rodders began to turn to more innocent looking coupes and sedans, particularly for their daily drivers. Later models of Ford V8

It doesn't have to be finished to be fun. For many early rodders, a rod was the only means of transportation, so it was driven daily in its unfinished state until such time as the work had been completed. This is rarer nowadays, as so many enthusiasts want that first outing to be in the completed car. These rodders clearly don't agree with that sentiment, and rightly so

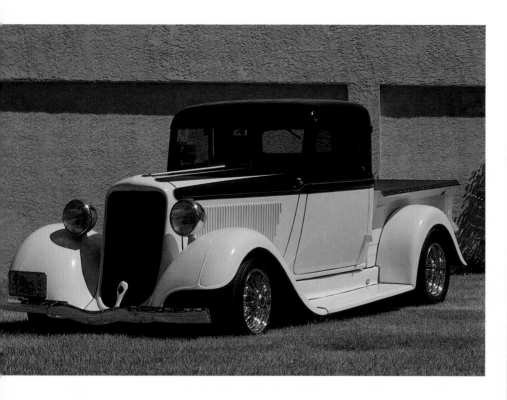

Above

A '34 Dodge pickup is rare indeed. This yellow and black beauty belongs to Stan Howerton from Rock Springs, Wyoming, who has owned it for ten years. Hustled by a stock 327 cu. in. Chevy V8, the truck rolls on Starwire wheels shod with Michelin tyres. The front end features a 4 in. dropped axle from Butch's Rod Shop with '54 Chevy spindles and brakes, and Vega steering. At the back, a '75 Chevy rear axle has been hung on stock springs from the Dodge chassis. All the chassis work was carried out by Tom Ligget, while that two-tone and scalloped paint was laid on by Carl Brunson, who also straightened out the bodywork. This included shaving the grille ornament and door handles, and adding a solid roof insert

Right

The interior of Stan Howerton's Dodge pickup was handled by MB's Custom Upholstery in Rock Springs. They stitched the black naugahyde seat and door covers and laid the carpeting. The steering wheel is a Cal Custom product

Left
Lafayette, Indiana, is the home town of this lime green '37 Ford pickup, which belongs to Ed and Noni Selleck. They, too, have followed the current trend away from chrome trim and towards an integrated colour scheme. Apart from the orange wheels that set the truck off nicely, everything is painted green, including the door handles and windshield wipers

Right
What could be nicer than bowling along in a '34 Ford cabriolet, the tyres singing and the wind blowing through your beard? This super-straight street rod is simple, but effective, the five-spokes setting off the black paint a treat. Note the down in front stance aided by 'big and little' tyres

Below right
If you're worried about rock chips, then fit your rod with a custom 'bra' to protect the front end paintwork. This blue flamed '39 Ford coupe is a tidy car—nothing outrageous, nothing hi-tech, just a good, solid street rod

Running red lights! This '35 Chevy and trailer certainly have plenty of tail lights. Note the nifty use of a spare set of rear fenders and rear panel on the trailer, plus the matching wire wheels

received their attention, too, but few other makes.

Fortunately, wiser members among the hot rodding movement urged the authorities to set aside areas where the rodders could race their cars legally, and eventually this led to the setting up of dragstrips, usually on abandoned wartime airports. At last rodders could cut loose without falling foul of the law.

For a while, the hot rods continued as dual-purpose cars. During the week they were driven to work and provided the rodder with his only form of transport; at the weekends they were driven to the strip or the dry lakes to race. Soon, however, towards the end of the 1940s, in the quest for ever more speed, it was no longer practical for the car to be used for both purposes. The pure competition car had arrived. Rodders still wanted 'hot' street wheels, however, and the street rod was born. This followed the style of the earlier hot rods, but gradually it became less austere and more showy. Roadsters were still very big, but coupes and sedans were growing in popularity,

particularly as many rodders were married and had growing families
in need of suitable transport.

Fords were still predominant and, indeed, still are today some 40
odd years later, but eventually other makes began to be modified.
Often this was as a result of their success on the dragstrips. Henry's
V8 continued to be big news until well into the 1950s, but in 1955 it
suffered a blow from which it was never to recover—the introduction
of the overhead-valve smallblock Chevrolet V8—still among the most
popular of street rod powerplants today.

Rodding itself continued to be popular until the mid-1960s, when it
was dealt a blow that left only the real died-in-the-wool enthusiasts
still building cars. In 1965, Ford introduced the Mustang—a factory
hot rod if ever there was one. No longer was it necessary to scrounge
parts and spend long hours in the garage constructing a performance
car. Now you could buy one from your local Ford dealer—the muscle
car era had arrived. GM followed with the Camaro and Firebird, then

*Black and flames still make an effective
paint scheme for any rod, as this '40 Ford
coupe, belonging to Don Prokop from Ohio,
proves. The car sits nice and low and has
some interesting features, such as the nosed
hood and painted grille sides. However, Don
chose not to go the modern 'dechromed'
route and retained the brightwork around
the headlights*

Overleaf
*A '36 Ford five-window with the modern
smoothie look produces a neat, understated
rod. The striping provides a little lift to the
black paint, and you have to look twice to
notice that there are no door handles*

Above

'When you grow up, you can have one just like it.' Street rodders often catch the bug young, and here's one would-be rodder who's impressed by the flawless paintwork on Mike Strusiasui's chopped '40 Ford coupe. The car is impressive from every angle . . .

Right

. . . as you can see in this view of the engine compartment. Under all those carburettors and the blower sits a well-detailed flathead V8. The car runs permanently without a hood—well, if you've got it, flaunt it!

Black with pink and blue flames is an interesting and eye-grabbing switch on an old idea. The nose of this chopped '29 Model A Ford sits down in the weeds thanks to a dropped I-beam axle. The painted grille shell is in tune with current trends, and the dropped headlight bar helps to make the car look low at the front

came the Dodge Charger. Street rodding was at an all-time low.

However, salvation was at hand. As we moved into the 1970s, the muscle of those lean, taut factory hot rods began to turn to fat. They became overweight and emasculated by increasingly strict emissions requirements. Once more, enthusiasts began to look for another way of having fun with cars and they rediscovered street rodding.

The rest, as they say, is history. From the early 1970s, street rodding has grown and grown, and is now firmly established as a major automotive hobby. The photographs in this book will give you

some idea of how diverse the styles of car are, but no matter whether a rodder builds a car that is an exact replica of one that was built in the 1940s—buggy springs, flathead V8 and all—or one that is a hi-tech piece of engineering with the very latest in suspension and engine technology, there is one overriding aim. That aim is to have fun with cars, something street rodders succeed in doing admirably.

A chopped Model A Tudor makes a great family street rod, and when you add a trailer, you've got a rod suitable for some long-distance running

Chrome yellow and baby blue scallops make for a stunning combination on this '37 Ford. Apart from the wheels, there is no brightwork at all, which works well, but don't step on those running boards. Vee'd windshield is a nice touch

Overleaf
In the pink! Mark Leduc's '40 Ford is a stunner in more ways than one. The pro-street coupe displays many interesting features, such as the pancaked hood, rounded door corners and lack of door handles. A blown motor provides the urge, while at the back, monster tyres have been tucked under the fenders

Apart from the colour, this pro-street '40
coupe is a virtual clone of Mark Leduc's
rod—pancaked hood, rounded door corners,
no rain gutters, no door handles. It's a prime
example of the pro-street look; notice how
those monster rear tyres are tucked way
under the rear

A '48 Chevrolet sedan delivery makes an unusual fat-fendered rod. The long and low hauler is powered by a 350 Chevy V8

Overleaf
Fat-fendered rods have become very popular recently, and they don't come much fatter fendered than Brad Davies' '47 Oldsmobile Sedanette. The car would be equally at home with later-model customs and exhibits many traditional custom touches—frenched lights, filled seams, dechroming, rounded door tops, chopped top and vee'd windshield. It also sits lo-o-ow!

Above
Pinks and baby blues are definitely the most fashionable colours at the moment, but is Harlen Neagle from Houston, Texas, a closet pinko? He skilfully used pink to detail the smallblock Chevy V8 in his otherwise baby blue '34 Chevy coupe. The engine features tuned-port injection

Above right
Ken and Mary Stek from Oskaloosa, Iowa, have given their green scalloped, red '37 Chevrolet pickup a competition look. The fenderless, bedless truck features independent front suspension and a monster wing over the rear axle to keep the tyres firmly in contact with the tarmac

Right
Plenty of polishing needed under the hood of Gene Younk's '40 Ford convertible

A fine example of the 'smoothie' look, Terry Markee's '34 Chevrolet coupe is a sharp looker. Note the one-piece hood top, recessed louvres in the hood side panels and the lack of door handles. A thin pinstripe provides an accent to the belt line

Overleaf
They don't get much lower. This wild '46 Chevy coupe is what fat-fendered rods are all about. Note the complete lack of any chrome or stainless trim and the few inches between the road and the front pan. The top has been chopped radically and the windshield glass butted together. One fascinating feature is the rear lip of the hood which has been flared upwards to conceal the windshield wipers when they are parked

Left

So pink, it hurts your eyes just to look at it—a pro-street coupe collects admiring glances from some junior rodders. Note the '39 Ford teardrop lights with bluedots and painted rims. The '37 Ford carries an apt licence plate

Above

Early Mopars are a long way behind in the street rod popularity stakes when compared with Fords and, latterly, Chevys. Even so, they can make neat cars, as shown by this Dodge coupe, which has been given the smoothie look. Pink and grey graphics give an accent to that white paint

Left

Motivation for Doug Gray's Willys is provided courtesy of a 454 cu. in. rat motor, which really fills that narrow engine compartment—note those reflections in the firewall. The exhaust is taken care of by means of zoomie headers fitted with marine baffles

Below

Doug Gray's '33 Willys hiboy convertible is one of a kind, since the factory never made them that way. Doug built his from a coupe, removing the roof, making the aluminium windshield posts and tubbing the wheelwells himself. A three-piece hood was fabricated by Rootlieb, while Howdy Ledbetter made the top and handled the interior. The bright Porsche red rod from Alamo, California, has an all-tube chassis that Doug made himself. He is also responsible for the independent front suspension, which is based on a pair of McPherson struts—rare indeed for any street rod. A Dana 60 rear end, suspended on Koni coil-overs and fitted with Currie disc brakes, turns those 28 in. wide rear tyres

Left

Mean, green and clean—any sort of Packard is a very rare sight at a rod event; this '48 coupe belongs to Gordy Swartz and has been given the pro-street look. The car is so fat and low that you can hardly see those monster rear tyres

Below

Randy High's '34 Chevy roadster shows that you don't need a Ford to build a hiboy. The cute mauve and pink scalloped rod has a smooth three-piece hood and, unusually, a dropped tube front axle mounted on coil-overs rather than a more traditional leaf spring

Left
The simple, clean and tidy interior in Rich
Malinowski's '32 Ford loboy roadster. Note
the unusual steering wheel and engraving.
Lettering on dash hints at what lies under
the hood

Above
The Maserati engine in Rich Malinowski's
'32 Ford. You need shades just to look at all
that gold plate and chrome!

Above left
Gary Ege, from Dixon, Illinois, owns this sharp orange '34 Chevy roadster. Tasteful graphics and the smoothie look produce a very sanitary street rod

Left
Street rod woodies are rare, but now and again one turns up, making the point that wood is good. This orange '33 Ford combines the modern smoothie look with traditional lacquered wood panelling. There's a whole lot of work in restoring that woodwork and keeping it looking good. Just one thing, where are the surf boards?

Above
This fully-fendered, turquoise '32 Ford roadster has some unusual vents in the sides of its three-piece hood, which have been accentuated by the graphics. The paintwork is very much in line with current trends towards pastel colours, but the wind-wings on the windshield posts and the stock bumpers are more in tune with the much earlier resto-rod theme. That's the great thing about street rodders—they are all individuals and don't necessarily slavishly follow any particular style, but mix and match to suit their own likes and dislikes

Left

For years '40 Willys coupes entertained the fans at the dragstrips; now they are finding a new lease of life as pro-street rods. This beautiful orange example is typical of the breed—dumped in front with the wheels tucked right up inside the fenders, tubbed wheelwells to contain huge rear tyres, and a parachute for some added braking power

Above

Here's a car that really means business—note the blower protruding from the hood and the rollcage visible inside. Wanna race?

You don't see many '38 Ford Tudor street rods, but here's one that proves that they can make wild rides. Those hot pink flames and the radically lowered lid make a head-turning combination. Check out the vee'd windshield and filler cap door in the rear fender

Right
At a glance, this burgundy coloured '38 Chevy coupe, belonging to Richard Maples, from Knoxville, Tennessee, seems a fairly run-of-the-mill street rod, but look closer. Those pink and blue graphics and the blower peeking out from under the hood suggest otherwise

Overleaf
As street rods, Willys coupes always look as though they are ready to race. This chrome yellow '40 is a prime example and is owned by Greg and Barb Dummer from Minnetonka, Minnesota

Above
Now here's an interesting rig—a street rod hauler complete with matching '32 Ford three-window coupe

Above right
How about this for fat fenders? One thing the fat-fendered fad has achieved is to bring a large number of unusual cars out of the woodwork. In years gone by, no rodder would have considered such material, but now these huge coupes and sedans are becoming very popular. This one's a '39 Buick, and it's been given the smoothie treatment by Tony Cooper from Wheaton, MO. Just look at that mail-slot windshield

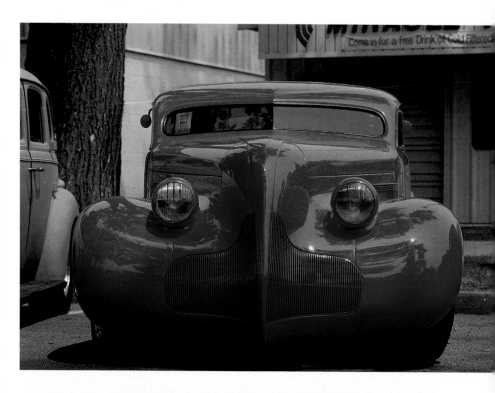

Right
Here's one to rattle the doors as it drives by—Bob Sargis' '40 Willys truck has the smoothie pro-street look and the muscle to go with it. The straight silver paint accentuates the powerful look of the pickup

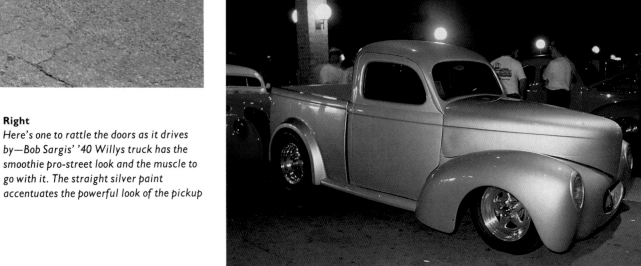

Above

Gayle Dorschner from Denver, Colorado, gives a final polish to her '33 Plymouth five-window coupe. Apart from the five-spoke wheels and shocking pink paint, the car is very much a resto-rod. Note that Gayle is colour co-ordinated with the car!

Above right

Quick, pass the sunglasses. Clyde Sutherland's hot pink '35 Chevy three-window coupe is a dazzler, and no mistake. The graphics and smoothie look go well with this Pennsylvania-based rod

Right

Providing a splash of colour is this hammered '34 Ford two-door sedan—makes a change from flames and the geometric precision of scallops

Above

The spotless engine compartment in Boyd Harwan's brilliant yellow '40 Ford coupe. There's a smallblock Chevy somewhere under all that glitter

Left

In recent years, street rodders have taken to creating body styles that were never produced by the manufacturers. Some of these 'phantom' bodies are now being produced in fibreglass, but here is one that is unique—a '32 Ford phaeton delivery

Far left

There was a time when no self-respecting rodder would have painted his '32 Ford hiboy roadster pink, but look at this one—notice the blower under the hood? The pale blue '34 Ford three-window coupe in the background is typical of the current smoothie trend, while the yellow '40 has a more traditional appearance

Above

Bill Quimby's '37 Ford club cabriolet originally started life as a club coupe, but was turned into a convertible by Ted Zgrzemski, who also built the car originally. The Frost beige lacquered street rod has the smoothie look so popular at the moment. It is powered by a stock 305 cu. in. Chevy backed by a Turbo 350 transmission, which is connected to a Maverick rear axle. This is hung on parallel leaf springs. At the front, Mustang II front suspension, brakes and power steering have been slotted under the flawless bodywork, while Cragar Drag Star wheels, shod with Goodyear rubber, have been fitted all round

Right

The interior of Bill Quimby's cabriolet features Pontiac Sunbird seats, re-upholstered in beige wool and leather, the same materials being used on the door panels. The custom-built dash contains Chevy van instruments, while the steering wheel is a LeCarra item

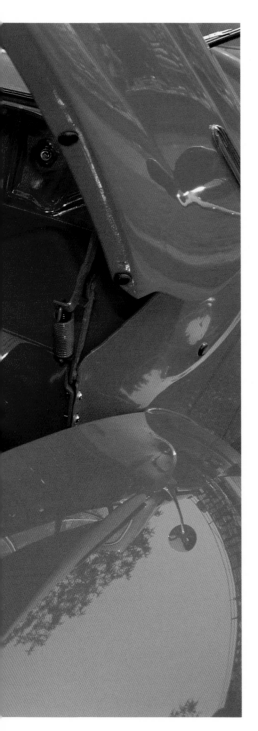

Left
The engine in Gene Waggener's Kansas-based rod features tuned-port injection. Everything about the car is spotless

Above
The interior of Gene Waggener's '40 Ford convertible has been designed for comfortable cruising. The tasteful, biscuit-coloured upholstery is matched by the steering wheel and vizors

Left
Close-up of the graphics on the side of the Stanifer's '37 sedan. Surprising what you can achieve with a little paint and imagination

Above
When it came to desirable body styles for building street rods, '37 Ford two-door sedans used to come a long way down the list. Now, attitudes have changed, and with the move into fat-fendered rodding, the '37 Ford has gained a new popularity. This pretty two-tone example belongs to Gary and Connie Stanifer from Whiteland, Indiana. Although very few changes have been made to the body—and most of those are limited to painting the chrome bits—the look is very effective

Above
Talk about radical. This is Chuck Reimer's '48 Buick Roadmaster. The car is super-long, super-wide and super-low. It is the epitome of the fat-fendered, smoothie street rod. That pastel turquoise paint is highlighted by pink and yellow graphics

Below
Reimer's Roadmaster has been seriously chopped, which simply accentuates its length and low stance all the more

Overleaf
In the search for ever different paint schemes, rodders are coming up with all manner of ideas. These are very definitely liquid assets

This '34 Ford five-window coupe is pretty
wild—check out the moulded fenders,
recessed grille and hood side panel. Those
carburettors have really got to restrict
vision through that narrow windshield

John Cassidy's '32 Ford three-window receives some well-deserved attention. The pastel blue hiboy coupe has some nice touches, including the smooth three-piece hood and vee'd front spreader bar. See the turn signals set into the bar? 'Big and little' rubber ensures the right stance

Rick Sawyer's rod is a fine example of a '39
Ford convertible. The deep black ragtop has
some interesting graphics in pink and blue.
The rod is up to the minute in the smoothie
fat-fendered style, everything being painted
rather than plated. Note the pancaked hood

There's plenty of polished aluminium under
the hood of Rick Sawyer's convertible. He
can open and close the hood automatically
by radio control, the trick being to sit nearby
and wait for some unsuspecting onlooker to
get close to the car, then pop the hood—
provides hours of entertainment

Left
The interior of Gary Ramsey's phaeton features Porsche 944 seats trimmed in tan leather with velour insets. The steering wheel is a LeCarra item

Below left
Gary Ramsey comes from Boulder, Colorado, and his neat '30 Ford Model A phaeton is based on a set of narrowed '32 Ford rails. The cute white and red scalloped hiboy hustles to the tune of a blown 302 cu. in. Ford V8 backed by a C4 automatic transmission. A ten-bolt Chevy axle has been installed at the rear with four-bar radius rods, while at the front there is a 5 in. dropped Magnum tube axle with Ford spindles carrying finned Buick brake drums

Below
The rear panel of the Model A body has been cut away to expose the stock transverse leaf spring and quick-change cover on the axle. The rod rolls on Super Slot wheels shod with Goodrich rubber

This pale blue '34 Ford coupe has some interesting features, including the painted grille shell, chopped roof, lack of rain gutters and the scoop formed at the rear of the three-piece hood. Independent front suspension is tucked well out of view under the front fenders

Here's another '40 Willys coupe that really means business

Coming.... This yellow '40 Ford convertible has the smoothie, painted look so popular now. Sits down in the weeds where it needs to be

Going. . . . A trio of rear ends. Presumably, tubbed wheelwells make that rumble seat unusable

Above
No matter what trends may come and go in rodding, chopped tops and flamed paint jobs will always be around. Patrick Huels' '37 Chevy two-door proves just that

Right
Gary Diercks from Muscatine, Iowa, owns this mouse-motored T-bucket. Note the satin-finished, milled aluminium goodies on the smallblock Chevy engine. The milled recesses have been picked out with colour to match the body and chassis. The paint-splattered pattern on the scuttle has also been copied in the back panel of the seat. Can you spot the front turn signals?

Left

That stack of Weber carburettors atop the
Ford V8 in Steven Pett's bright yellow '41
Ford is more than enough to attract your
attention, as is the spotless engine
compartment. However, should you tire of
gazing at all that glitter, check out the
mural under the hood - a montage of scenes
and characters from the movie American
Graffiti

Above

From deep in the heart of Texas, this black
and green '35 Ford two-door slantback is a
tidy looking street rod. Note the unusual
division between the colours and the colour
co-ordinated wheel centres. It's amazing the
effect that colour combinations can have on
an otherwise stock body

Left

When you build special-interest vehicles and manufacture street rod parts for a living, your own rod has to be something special, since it becomes a rolling advertisement for your business. This is just the case with Ken Fenical's '32 Ford club sport coupe, as Ken is proprietor of Posies, the well-known street rod company. The cream yellow rod sits down in the weeds thanks to a dropped axle and four-bar set-up at the front. At the rear there is an 8 in. Ford axle on a Posies super-slide spring, and the car rolls on Real wheels all round with Goodrich tyres. The body started life as a fibreglass three-window coupe, but Ken's company removed the roof and carried out the necessary modifications to turn it into a ragtop. These included reshaping the tops of the doors and removing the sill from the windshield

Below left

Ken Fenical's '32 Ford is powered by an essentially stock 351 Ford V8 backed by a C4 automatic transmission. It's unusual to see a street rod engine with virtually no chromed or polished aluminium goodies. The air conditioning was provided by Vintage Air

Below

The interior of the club sport coupe is an excellent example of Posies' workmanship, the upholstery being carried out in a combination of vinyl and cloth. The front seats are from a Toyota, while the steering wheel is an AMX item. The wood-veneered dash was carried out by Cumberland Woodcraft

Overleaf

Scallops were once as popular as flames for a custom paint job, but they fell from favour for a while and are only just beginning to be popular again. This pink and black '41 Ford shows just how effective they can be. Note the smoothie look with a complete lack of any hood ornamentation together with the frenched headlights

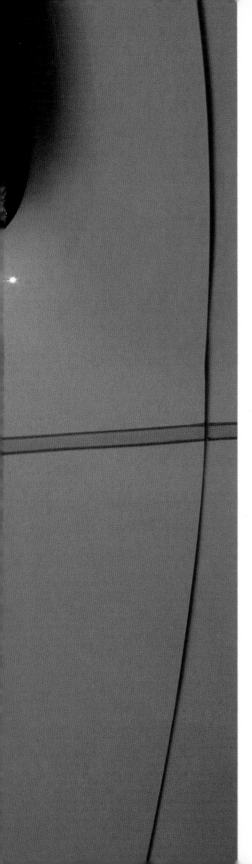

Left

You hardly ever see a Lincoln street rod, but Ron Schmidt's pro-street coupe more than makes up for their rarity. This little doodle appears on the door

Above

Don't get too close—it may bite! The '41 Lincoln coupe is a fitting end to this book. It's right on the money in terms of being at the very leading edge of the current ultimate street rod trend. It's pink and baby blue, it's fat fendered, it has the smoothie look, and it's a pro-street monster with more than enough muscle to hold its own on the dragstrip. Such cars may not be totally practical for travelling long distances, but they show that the spirit of the early hot rodders still lives on, and once again dual-purpose street and competition machines are being built

Overleaf

Welcome to street rod city